AN
Echoing
Call

God's call echoes through the years.

Marcy

Marcy Keefe-Slager

To Mother Mary
and the Blessed Trinity
for Their faithfulness and Their calls

CONTENTS

FOREWORD

I am one of Marcy Keefe-Slager's friends and "spiritual soul sisters." We come from different Christian backgrounds, but this has never been an obstacle in our faith sharing. At present, I am sitting on my balcony with my heart full from rereading Marcy's book, *An Echoing Call.* I have been contemplating what I can say in this foreword that will do justice to the powerful way God speaks through Marcy's life and writing. My mind drifts off as I sit waiting for wisdom and I realize I am staring at the neatly laid terra-cotta tiles around my feet.

The tiles are perfectly laid: nicely square with perfect grout lines outlining the tiles. As I admire the tiles with my artistic eye, I realize there is an odd deviation in the tile layout. For some reason those who laid the tile decided to cut right through the perfect grid of squares with a diagonal line of grout. My eye follows this diagonal line, pondering why it was put there. It doesn't seem to be repairing any defect in the tiles because the tiles transected by the narrow diagonal line of grout are as perfectly cut as the rest. I find the answer to my musing: the diagonal line of grout leads directly to the drainage pipe. When rain pours down, this narrow line of grout serves its purpose by directing the water to the drainage pipe, where it pours off the balcony into the garden below. It's a small line of grout, but it must serve as a catalyst that changes the directional flow of the rain.

Now I'm inspired! Marcy's journey of pastoral and prophetic ministry seems so like this diagonal line of grout. She is a catalyst, placed by God in the midst of a hierarchical church structure. While she ponders why her priestly call cannot be honored by the Church, God uses His call on her life and ministry as a spiritual catalyst within the Church and outside it. He is certainly working in Marcy and speaking through her.

Once I was at a retreat day with Marcy. She had us reflect upon the words of Mary, the mother of Jesus: "I am a servant of the Lord; let this happen to me according to your word" (Luke 1:38 New English Translation [NET]). Though in this treasured passage of scripture, Mary expressed fear and concern and had questions; she surrendered herself to the ordination of God for her life's purpose. Marcy's writing is likewise full of observations, concerns, questions, and even fears, yet Marcy's writing documents her faith and her ability to see the underlying love of God. Like our Blessed Mary, Mother of God, Marcy's writing reveals that she, too, lives surrendered to the ordination of God for her life's purpose.

While Marcy has yearned to be part of God's ministry as a priest in the church hierarchy, I believe she has been ordained for a unique priestly and prophetic purpose. The fruit of her ministry and prophetic yearnings bear witness to her divine ordination. Her ministry has reached men and women from a number of religious traditions who yearned for a deeper understanding of God's love.

This book may be read through from cover to cover to gain understanding and inspiration from Marcy's journey. Whether you know Marcy or not, you will recognize the amazing love of God that is present in her writing. The Holy Spirit speaks through her poetic voice in each entry.

You may prefer to read this book more slowly, one poem at a time. My favorite way to read Marcy's work is to stay with a poem and savor it until it speaks to me. At times, it has seemed that the poem doesn't speak to my current situation, but I have found that even then the love and peace of the Holy Spirit unfolds within me, in much the same way that God speaks to me through the inspirational writing of the psalmists.

I thank Marcy for sharing her experience and insights with us. I pray that God will speak to you, the reader, as she shares the journey of how she has heard and struggled to follow the echoing call of God. May her courage to find her voice and speak in these pages give you hope and courage on your own journey.

Just as each one has received a gift, use it to serve one another as good stewards of the varied grace of God. Whoever speaks, let it be with God's words. Whoever serves, do so with the strength that God supplies, so that in everything God will be glorified through Christ Jesus. To him belong the glory and the power forever and ever. Amen.

(*1 Peter 4:10-11 NET*)
Bev Nemecek
Antigua, Guatemala
August 2011

Some would say it isn't possible,
it just can't be.
Yet, if they informed God,
God took no heed.
God's call has echoed
through the years.

PREFACE

In the first century Council of Jerusalem, the Church resolved the contentious issue of whether one had to convert to Judaism in order to become part of Christ's Church. Swaying that decision was the impact the baptism of the Holy Spirit was having upon Gentile converts. God was bestowing the Holy Spirit equally on Jew and Gentile alike.

In much the same way, God is inviting the Church to appreciate the call to priesthood that He is making to women like Marcy Keefe-Slager as an indication of His desire that ordination be a path open to both genders. I have been blessed, as Marcy's pastor, to have ministered beside her for nearly two decades. I've also been blessed to experience the spiritual lift that the poems of this book have provided me through the years. My faith journey has been fortified by Marcy's writings and our frequent conversations. Her love of the Catholic faith, her devotion to the sacraments, and the humble way she has accepted the wound of having her Church spurn the call she has been given are inspirations to me and so many others who call her spiritual director and friend.

Now in the last months of her earthly life, we also receive the thoughtful insights of one "sentenced" to carry in her body an aggressive cancer. Marcy has further opened her soul that we might see in her poetry the courageous face of suffering and acceptance. In my opinion, this is not a book that is meant to be read cover to cover in a short time. Each poem deserves to be savored, to be prayerfully discerned. If any of these poems offer consolation to those who are suffering or offer encouragement to girls and women who know they're hearing God's call to the priesthood, then this poet, I'm certain, will feel enriched beyond measure.

Fr. Jim Shaver
Pastor
St. John the Evangelist Church

ACKNOWLEDGMENTS

To all who have welcomed my ministry.

To all who have encouraged and

supported me in my journey.

To all who have helped me hear God's echoing call.

To all who have helped to bring this book to fruition.

To my spiritual mentors.

To all who give me life.

To my husband, Harv, and my dear friend Betty for attending to the details of publishing.

God's gifts and God's call are irrevocable.

Romans 11:29, New American Bible (NAB)

INTRODUCTION
MY JOURNEY

In the early 1960s when Pope John XXIII felt the need for the Catholic Church to make some major changes, I was skeptical. When he convened the Second Vatican Council, and bishops from around the world came together to define and develop these changes, I feared losing what I had gained in my spiritual life as a young Sister. Even though many saw these developments as a breath of fresh air to invigorate the Church, I complained that it sounded like too much change for the sake of change.

Some of my fears were quieted when I interacted with Sisters who were vibrant, joyful, and living examples of the Gospel. I learned that trading religious habits for secular garb did not mean shedding our identity or our Christianity. I was encouraged and eager to hear what was coming next. I could see the influence of the Holy Spirit in the Council's proclamations.

As I watched, waited, and wondered, I began to feel the cooling breezes of the "fresh air." It was exciting to think of the Church as something more than a hierarchical pyramid. The bishops were presenting a circular model where each member—laity, religious, and clergy—was integral to the community that formed the Body of Christ on earth. We each had our specific role in the Kingdom. Our community prayer—to truly be worship—required full, active, conscious participation of all in attendance. To facilitate this participation, the altar was turned around so that the priest faced the people. We were an expression of the Euchrist, joined together in song and prayer in our own language. Enthusiastically I became a Lector and a Eucharistic Minister. What a joy to be able to proclaim the Word of God to the community.

The new concepts in the documents of Vatican II played a significant role in bringing vibrancy into my faith and spirituality. Moving from the common existing model of preached retreats and rote prayer to a new model of directed retreats and the opportunity to share with a skilled person the movement of God in my life allowed me to have a whole new experience of God. God was no longer the exacting, judging God of my youth who kept careful records of my wrongdoings. More and more, through the years, I learned that God is the God of unconditional love, the God who embraces, invites, and forgives without reservation. How awesome it has become to know that God never says, "When you get it together—or—if you *ever* get it together, I will love you."

I was young and in a religious congregation of Franciscan women when this transformation in my spiritual life began. As I continued to grow into varying stages of maturity I realized that faith, God, and Church are not only my life, they are my passion! This passion grew as I immersed myself in the depths of prayer and ministry during my many years in the convent. As I prayed and served others, God was doing marvelous things in my soul by drawing me closer and closer. So much so that nothing gives me greater delight than being able to help others realize that they are near and dear to God—no ifs, ands, or buts about it. The more I can help others experience this reality, the more joy I experience.

Many years in ministry led to the awesome privilege of being a hospital chaplain. After fourteen years of service, the hospital, in a downsizing effort, offered me early retirement, which I accepted. In the days following this transition, at age fifty-seven, I was still chomping at the bit to be involved in ministry. I wanted and needed to be active in ministry in my Church. Yet, I kept meeting all kinds of roadblocks. My suspicion was that I was found to be unsuitable because I had recently gotten a dispensation from my religious vows. A few years earlier I heard God tell me I needed to go in a new and different direction. I took God's message to say I was to leave the convent. The church readily granted my request for a dispensation from my vows. Some people, however, had accused me of being unfaithful to the Church. Little did they know I was responding to God's call. As I worked and prayed my way through this "new direction" there was peace in my soul.

Yet none of the rejection and discrimination directed at me made any sense. Through many tears and agonizing prayer, my spiritual director was able to help me find God in all these painful and confusing times. By this time I readily counted forty years of education, training, and ministerial experience. I had served as a teacher, an outreach minister to the Cherokee Nation in North Carolina, and a hospital chaplain. Intertwined in these opportunities was the grace that helped me grow in greater awareness of God's presence in the nuances of the nature of true ministry. I learned and grew as I assisted others in their life circumstances.

As I prayed, pondered, and questioned the rejection from my church leaders, my spiritual director asked if I was called to be a priest. It had to have been a question directly from the Holy Spirit. After a moment of stunned silence, all I could say was, "Yes! Yes! Yes!" Then came the memory from seventh grade in St. Boniface School in New Riegel, Ohio. Sister Clementia had urged us to take some of our recess time to go to Church and ask God what He would have us do with our lives. More than once, as I walked away from those visits, I almost floated in elation with the desire to be a priest.

However, way back in the early 1950's how was one to talk of such a call? I was a child and a female. Besides, there was never any mention made of such a possibility in Church or society. What was I to do with this elation? I must have translated it into a call to be a Sister because at the ripe old age of fourteen, I entered prep school with the Sisters of St. Francis of Tiffin, Ohio, where I continued to thrive for thirty years.

Through those many years I was enriched in more ways than I will ever comprehend. I received an excellent education, along with training and countless experiences of ministry and immersion in prayer and spirituality. Even more enrichment came my way as I experienced transition from religious life to being a member of the laity in the Church. What a revelation to learn that God loved me as much as a layperson as when I was a Sister.

As I searched for opportunities for ministry, I turned to my community in Jackson, Michigan. Involvement with Christian and non-Christian people broadened my appreciation for my own faith and that of my brothers and sisters. There is no end to the fresh air I now breathe as my husband and I continue to live our marital commitment to each other, a commitment that began seven years after I received my dispensation. Now, facing my mortality as I live with cancer brings new experiences of fresh air as you will find expressed in chapter five.

Over the years I have learned that the roadblocks, disappointments, and challenges of life have hidden blessings—when I allow myself to see them. As I work through the bumps and bruises, I have come to learn what I truly believe, what is most important to me. I truly believe that God is the God of love and that you and I are integral members of the Body of Christ. The Lord calls for our faithful participation in enlivening the Kingdom. It is important for me to be attentive to God's presence and love and to radiate that love to others so they too will flourish in God's love. It is important that I know our Gospel mandate to listen and follow Jesus' teaching and that I respond with all the energy I have.

As I strive to put these thoughts into a coherent message I rejoice in God's faithfulness to me and my yearning to be faithful in return. God's embrace gives me the strength and courage to live as fully as possible.

How is it possible that God can be present to me while there are so many tragic things happening in the world? Yet somehow I know without a doubt that regardless of all that is happening, God *is* with me. Though my Church leaders declare it is impossible for God to call a woman to priesthood, the desire continues to pulse through me. Along with this call is the one I have heard consistently from many sources through the years: to speak up, raise my voice, and proclaim what God is doing in my life.

The voices of encouragement, from leaders and colleagues, have grown more consistent and persistent in recent days. In an effort to give expression to God's call and guidance, prose has given way to the poetic form you will find in the following pages. These poetic reflections have been written over the last dozen years as I have relished God's ever-loving presence and love and the awe of being one of God's chosen. Some were written as I struggled with the direction today's hierarchy is leading the Church. A part of that struggle includes grappling with the differing voices and the polarization in the Church today. It feels like today's Church leaders are working hard to shut the windows opened by Pope John XXIII, the windows that let in the wonderful fresh air. Dealing with lung cancer (and no, I never, *ever* smoked), I am learning more than I ever wanted to know about being short of breath. As my body gasps for air to breathe, my spirit craves to be satiated with the fresh air introduced into my life through Vatican II. I yearn all the more that the Church that introduced me to refreshing ways of being will insist the windows be wide open.

Some of my poems give expression to the tension between what Pope John Paul II and his successor Pope Benedict XVI describe as God's will with regard to the ordination of women and what I have experienced as God's call and God's will. Some were written as meditations and reflections on the marvel of being held close to God. God's call to us is both vocational and relational. How awesome to have a God who repeatedly invites, "Come to Me."

One of my vocational calls is to priesthood, but I do not feel called to ordination in today's Church, where any mention of the ordination of women is considered a violation of Church doctrine. Fighting that battle would be a total distraction and much too exhausting at this time in my life. I would have little energy left to minister with God's people. Having said that, I rejoice in having had nearly fifty years in which to proclaim God's Word, though not from the pulpit, except those few precious times when I was with Isaiah Missions. What a thrill to have some of my Protestant friends invite me into their pulpits. My heart sings when I am privileged to teach a course in ministry in our Diocesan Formation Program. Though not permitted to preside at the Eucharist, the Lord has used me as a vessel to nourish others spiritually. Being a chaplain and a spiritual director has provided abundant opportunities to speak words of comfort, reassuring people of God's love, healing, and forgiveness.

Whether you are Catholic or of another faith, I tell my story because I yearn for us to turn our attention to the needs of the Kingdom that are crying for more laborers in the vineyard. I tell my story to encourage others to be attentive and to listen to God's echoing call and to respond.

God is not limited by our human guidelines and declarations.

Marcy Keefe-Slager
July 2011

Through the words of the Prophet Isaiah, ponder God's affirmation as spoken to you.

IN HONOR OF YOU, ONE OF GOD'S CHOSEN

(An adaptation of Isaiah 43, October 2010)

Now, thus says the Lord,
    who created you and formed you, O Beloved,
Fear not, for I have embraced you;
I have called you by name: you are Mine.
When you pass through the challenges of life,
    I will be with you.
When doubts and bewilderment taunt you,
    you shall not succumb,
        your spirit will be filled.
You are precious in My eyes
    and glorious. I love you.

You are My witness, My Beloved,
    My faithful one whom I have chosen
To know and believe in Me
    and understand that it is I.
    I call you forth.

See, I am doing something new!
    Now it springs forth, do you not perceive it?
In the desert of your unknowns I make a way,
    in your emptiness, rivers of fulfillment.
The people you have accompanied
    in their life's journeys
        I have formed for Myself,
        that they might announce My praise.
You, and they, shall proclaim,
        I am the Lord's!

✤ ✤ ✤

CHAPTER 1

ECHOES OF GOD'S CALL

There an angel of the Lord appeared to him {Moses} in fire flaming out of a bush.

Exodus 3:2

The Call

November 1999

It's amazing to realize—
  the Lord really ought to know better!
God continues to call,
   while His Vicar continues to protest,
  "No way! It's a matter of faith—
   validated by the Scriptures!
  There shall not even be discussion
   of the ordination of women."

It's truly hard to believe! I've denied it so long.
  It seemed so futile to acknowledge.
   To what avail?
Yet, the Lord's call, extended so many years ago,
   continues to echo within my soul.
  "I want you to proclaim My word.
   I need you to radiate My love.
  I yearn for you to herald My Presence.
   I grace you with My embrace.
  I call you to be Priest,
   one of my anointed ones."

Roman Catholic to the very depths of my being,
I am nurtured and nourished
by Word and Sacrament,
yet, God's gift of feminine body and spirit
is source of my Church's restriction.
It will feed me the Lord's Supper,
but will not allow me to stand at the Table.
Like so many other women, called,
I have creatively, faithfully responded
To my baptismal priesthood,
Even as the church contends it cannot,
Declares it will not,
Bestow Sacramental Orders.
Christ, my Lord, continues to call.

✡ ✡ ✡

Many Selves

December 2007

Born so many years ago,
 Second daughter to Thomas and Julia,
  humble farmers in Ohio.
 Younger sibling to Ruth Ann—
   gone before us into eternity—
  then came Adam, Roger and Martha.
 One of life's transitions led to marriage to Harv,
  of a very religious family on Long Island.
 Stepmother to John Mark and Elizabeth,
   fine young adults.
 Grandmother to Amelia and Miranda—
  no "steps" allowed here.

Friend to, and befriended by, innumerable people.

Woman of God,
 blessed beyond expectation.
Franciscan life,
 woven with life as teacher and chaplain.

Along with silver hair, coming more into my own,
        while being immersed in ministry,
        growing into more age
            and wisdom, hopefully, and grace.
   Though the hierarchy says it can't be so,
        yet, heard God's call to Priesthood
           amid a young girl's prayer.
  Gradually, slowly, eventually
        beginning to understand and accept—
          in more recent years—
  I live my Priesthood
      most freely,
      most effectively,
  as a laywoman in the Church.

Echoing

Water in the Desert

March 29, 2006

"For I put water in the desert...

for My chosen people to drink.

The people whom I formed for Myself

that they might announce My praise."

Isaiah 43:20–21

Yahweh our God proclaims,
"I put water in the desert of your souls...
    that you might drink deeply
        and know Me...
    that your thirst for Love
        may be satisfied and flourish...
    that you be filled with abundance
        and grace to share...
    that My Life may take root in you
        and spring forth in peace and justice...
    that you be empowered
        to further My Kingdom and
        to announce My Praise."

✤ ✤ ✤

Echoing

En Folded in Love

Love announced so long ago
    impregnated the maiden Mary
And quickened, upon meeting
    the spirit of cousin Elizabeth.
Love spoken then
    speaks yet today and always,
Beloved.

    My Son, My Daughter,
    I enfold YOU in My Love.
Know that you are filled with My grace,
    throbbing with My life.
I, your God, am with you always.
    Blessed are you and holy.
    Blessed is the fruit of your labors.
Bring to birth the love you bear.
As with Mary,
    love evokes heartfelt response.
My soul can't help but praise
    and magnify You, my Lord!
My spirit rejoices in You,
    for You, my God,
    are faithful and true.

✧ ✧ ✧

Echoing

Gospel Mandate

(Based on Matt. 28:18–20, Rom. 11:29,
and an adaptation of Isa. 43)

January 2006

My Beloved,
Know that your gifts—God's gifts to you-—
    that your call—God's call to you-—
        are irrevocable.
    They are nonrefundable.
    I can't take them back.
Go, therefore, into the world,
        along with your ordained brothers,
    and make disciples for My Kingdom.
Embrace My people
    in arms and hearts of LOVE—
    teach them,
    care for them,
    reassure them of God's love.
Support and love one another
    as you labor together in My vineyard.
And remember—
    You are precious in My Eyes.
    I love you.
    I call you by name.
    I am with you in the fire and flood.
    Know that I am with you always!

✤ ✤ ✤

CHAPTER 2

BUILDING THE KINGDOM

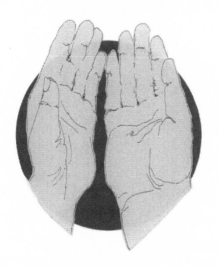

Peace is my farewell to you, my peace is my gift to you; I do not give it to you as the world gives peace. Do not be distressed or fearful.

John 14:27

Echoing

Envisioning The Kingdom

May, 2001

Our CALL:
SERVE God's people—all of them.
The Lord's MANDATE:
GO FORTH into the world—every corner.
Our MISSION:
PROCLAIM God's WORD—with conviction.
The VISION:
ENFLESH God's LOVE—within and around.
RECEIVE God's WORD,
BRING to birth.
HONOR the Call,
UTILIZE every talent.
EMPOWER the laborers,
SELECT the tools.
SWING OPEN the gates,
DISMISS doubt and fear.
PLANT the seeds,
GLEAN the harvest.
CELEBRATE each grace,
COMMUNE with God.
VISION—
incarnated by ACTION—
BIRTHS the Kingdom of God.

✡ ✡ ✡

Rebuild My Church

Retreat, May 2005

"What could You want of *me?*"
  rose the anguish from the depths of his being.

"Francis," the Voice from the Crucifix cried in response,
  "Go and rebuild My Church,
    which you see, is falling to ruin."

The cry from the Crucifix
  echoes through the centuries, even to today.
    "Rebuild My Church!"

Brick by brick, stone by stone,
  heart to heart, hand to hand,
    "Rebuild My Church."

"See with contemplative, prayerful eye
  My wounds in each Samaritan
    beaten, misunderstood,
      neglected by the roadside of life.

Reach out with My Love,
  embrace those foreign and near
    as you would embrace Me.

Generously pour in the balm
of acceptance and understanding
tenderly apply bandages
of forgiveness and mercy,
embrace with blessing.

Let your love be as sustaining
as Mine is to you,"
pleads the God of Love.

Rebuild, restore, renew
My Body,
My Church.

✡ ✡ ✡

Attending to the Spirit

(A reflection spun from "Presiding Skills for Prayer and Worship" taught by James Empereur, S.J.)

May 2002

"Before you preside or teach or preach,
    ATTEND to your SPIRITUALITY,"
      so urged the instructor.
Know your stuff,
      but most of all, KNOW the SPIRIT.

Be AWARE of God's ever-loving PRESENCE.
    EMBRACE God's DESIRE for you.
Be EMBRACED by God's LOVE.

PONDER the WORD.
      DRINK deeply of the CUP.
    Be NOURISHED so you can NOURISH.

ATTEND to the WHOLE of your BEING.
    REPLENISH your LAMP
      with the OIL of LOVE—
      wholesome SELF-LOVE
        that laughs and cries,
        plays and works,
        wakes and sleeps,
        relishes solitude and community.

Know WHO you are,
    and WHOSE you are.
Your God certainly knows YOU,
    and is CRAZY about you.

✫ ✫ ✫

Echoing

We Are the Body of Christ

September 2000

We are the Body of Christ—
    Women,
        Men,
            Children
        Laity,
            Religious,
                Ordained
Called,
    "Come to me
        ALL of you!
    Touch,
        Hold,
            Partake."
    Held sacred
            By our God
        Holding sacred—
                In hand and heart—
Sacred Vessels
    Made precious,
        Reverenced,
            Revered,

Even as we
    Reverence,
        Revere
            The Body of Christ.

✡ ✡ ✡

Echoing

Feed on Me

September 2003

"Take and eat,
    This is My Body..."
Jesus invites, yearns, commands.

Take. Reach out. Satisfy your hunger...
    with open hands,
        open heart,
        open spirit.
Eat. Chew this Food. Feed on Me...
    savor each Morsel,
    glean each Nutrient,
    ingest each Sacred Particle.
This is My Body...
    Word made Flesh
        proclaiming God's Love
    commanding love in return
        for neighbor, for self,
        for peace, for justice,
        for all on mother earth.

This is My Body...
    broken and risen,
        healing balm for your wounds,
            food for your soul.
Don't just eat.
    Chew, chew this Food!
        Feed on Me,
Then feed my people!

✡ ✡ ✡

Echoing

Differing Voices

2009

The SPIRIT became vibrant and exciting
   in the days following the Second Vatican Council.
No longer exacting and punishing,
     with Heart and Arms wide open,
    God embraces:
      "You are precious in my eyes!"
      "You are a pearl of great price."
      "You are mine. I love you!"
      "Go, and proclaim My Love!"

But, Whoa!
Some, with differing approaches
     to God and Church,
     cry, "WHOA!"
With great authority they chastise,
      "Where is your reverence?
      The Lord can be contained only
        in vessels of gold, or maybe silver.
      Then, bow down in reverence!
      Be ever so reverent!
      Be ever so reverent!
      You must be ever so reverent!"

To my aching heart
the SPIRIT of my LOVING GOD
     says "Live!
     Be at peace, My daughter, My loved one!
     Be RADIANT!
     Reverence ME in all that I have created!"

✬ ✬ ✬

The Ache

God's and the People's

August 2007

The Church, the Body of Christ—
    so vital, yet dwindling,
        so vibrant, yet floundering,
            meant to be One, yet polarizing.
My heart, my soul aches for my Church!

In centuries past, St. Jerome's ache for God's people
    led to translation of Scripture
        into "the vulgar" language
    enabling God's people to read, to hear, to know,
        to live God's WORD.

In more recent years, Members of Vatican II,
    responsive to the Spirit of Christ,
        called God's People to
    "full, active, conscious participation" in liturgy,
        as if to say,
    "People of God, LIVE what you PRAY!
        PRAY what you LIVE!"

My heart, my soul leapt in exhilaration!
    I came to know God as alive, caring, present,
        the God of all.

Now, the International Commission
        on English in the Liturgy
    proposes confusing words,
        fidelity to literal translation,
            not the Spirit of the Gospel!

My heart, my soul yearns for more for my church!

God's call to fidelity
    far exceeds rituals and ancient vocabulary!
God invites ALL, not just "the many"
    to intimacy, to salvation,
        to living as the Body of Christ—
  "Full, active, conscious participation"
    brings God's WORD to LIFE!
ALL of us!
    EACH of us!
      "Full, active, conscious participation!"
My heart, my soul aches for my Church!

Imagine

February 2011

As we journeyed through
    our Mission Awareness Trip in India
we all spoke English—
    directors, translators, sponsors.
Yet, their English was not quite like ours,
    ours not quite like theirs.

Ears were not tuned to pick up nuances,
    tongues not trained to speak more distinctly,
        to choose more descriptive words,
    conversants reluctant to persist
        until there was understanding.
Too often attempted conversations ended
    with a silent nod,
        diverted eyes,
        unanswered questions.

Imagine the impact of more creative persistence,
    the depth of communication,
        the expanse of understanding
    if we had been more courageous,
            more creative,
        in plumbing the possibilities.

Imagine the possibilities in the Kingdom
    when we truly plumb the depths of God's WORD
        and courageously proclaim IT to the world.

✫ ✫ ✫

Echoing

Divine Presence

September 2000

Loving PRESENCE
    In Bread and Wine
        Church—Christ's Body
           Assembly of God's people
                Each and every person
Faith-filled eye
    Knows Christ in the Tabernacle.
        Reverent knee bends
Oft veiled in recognition
    Of that same LOVE
        In Spouse,
           Parent,
                Child.
        Brother
        Sister
Divine Presence—
    Awesome,
        Unseen.
           Help us to see.

✿ ✿ ✿

CHAPTER 3

LIFE'S JOURNEY

The Lord preceded them in the daytime by means of a column of cloud to show them the way, and at night by a column of fire to give them light.

Exod. 13:21

Thoughts on Transition

May 1999

(Isaiah. 41&43)

Transitions!
Sometimes we are eager and ready to welcome them.
Sometimes we want nothing more than to stay put.
  Sometimes we are excited.
  Sometimes we are bitter
    because of the unfairness of life.
Yet, all of life is a transition.
  We are born to grow and to develop.
We journey through our ever-changing life,
  moving to that moment of ultimate transition,
    to our heavenly home.
Our life of transition is patterned in God's Word
  as the Scriptures spell out
    the journey of God's people
      through the Story of Salvation.
The Chosen People traveled
      over mountains and through deserts.
  There were times of peace and exaltation,
    and times of exile, pain, and war.
Daily we experience bits and pieces
  of the Paschal Mystery of Jesus.
As He lived, suffered, died, and rose to new life,
    so do we.
Jesus' fidelity to His mission
      of proclaiming His Father's love
  brought Him both rewards and suffering.

Hence, the story of our lives and our ministries.
Many people respond
        to our proclamation of God's love.
Many have hardened their hearts and cast stones.
Through the prophet Isaiah,
                Yahweh, our God, reassures us,
"Fear not, I am with you...
        For I am the Lord, your God,
                who grasp your right hand.
        It is I who say to you,
                'Fear not, I will help you.'
        I have called you by name: you are mine.
        When you pass through the water
                        I will be with you;
                in the rivers you shall not drown.
        Remember not the events of the past,
                        the things of long ago consider not.
                        See I am doing something new!
        Now it springs forth, do you not perceive it?"
Our mission in all of our transitions is to love,
        as our God loves us.

✧ ✧ ✧

Winter Times

October 1999

In the class on death and dying
      a woman spoke of her severest teacher—
her divorce, and all the harsh realities
      she was forced to accept.

Winter is one such teacher.
Interspersed with brilliant sunshine
      glittering on freshly fallen snow,
we are accosted with darkness
        and unknown perils
        of unpredictable hazards.
Bitter, biting cold
    chills every fiber of our being.
Blizzards blur our vision
    and endanger our travel.
Snow, sleet, and ice obstinately
    dare us to clear a path for ourselves.
There seems no way to escape
    barrenness and austerity on every side.
All of life, or so it seems,
    is snarled in relentless obstacles.

Yet, deep down inside,
in the midst of our desolation,
we know there is still light and life.
Just as with the winter wheat and the crocuses,
gathering energy
to burst through the ice and snow,
so our spirits desperately cling to
the promise and hope of spring.

Though at times harsh, or even cruel,
our winter experiences bring forth
unknown reserves of strength and resolve.
We come to the realization
we have not traversed this hazardous road alone.
The One who lovingly came to earth
to live as we do,
who accepted death
in consequence for His fidelity,
brings us, once again, to New Life.

Just a Scratch

July 2006

A vehicular squeal up ahead gave warning—
    Stay back! Make way!
But how? Trapped between the car behind
    and the truck rolling backward,
        downhill toward me.
Wait and watch,
    paralyzed with helplessness,
    for metal to crumple metal!

Journey from church to home
    veered from police report
        to insurance estimates
        to bodywork adjustments
        to rental car entanglements.
Inconvenience unannounced became
    a gut-wrenching ache of injustice
    when rental agency demanded,
    "How do you plan to pay
        for the scratch on the door!?"
What scratch? "But I didn't put it there!
    It's not my fault!"

'Twas a jumble of circumstances—
    backed-up traffic,
    truck's bad brakes,
    mysterious scratch—
all so minimal, so insignificant.

Just a scratch of injustice—
    witnessed too often,
in the face of truly gut-wrenching
    disturbances and discriminations—
        over a person's skin color,
        differing religious beliefs,
        sexual orientation,
        hunger for power,
        genocide,
        abject poverty…

Reflections spawned by a gut churned
    by just a scratch.

The Road to Hana

July 2000

Hana, a tiny town
     nestled on the coast of Maui,
  invites sojourners
    to venture
on a memorable journey.

The Road to Hana—
     oh so like life:
  innumerable curves,
     terrifying turns,
exhilarating heights,
    blinding lows,
straight, smooth paths,
    scraping mountainside,
precarious cliffs,
    washboard roads,
jolting bumps,
    screaming dips,
       thrilling views.

Tour guide points out
    waterfalls and flora,
        rainbow eucalyptus,
    volcanic residue,
        escapades of movie stars.

Ours is the journey
    of grandeur and fear,
        excitement and danger,
    awesome beauty,
        rugged challenges,
    always in the reassuring Presence
        of the Divine Tour Guide.

✭ ✭ ✭

Margins

Sabbath Retreat, May 10, 2005

It was in the margins of life and Church,
    and in the marginalized, that Francis and Clare,
        and so many others, found God.
            So with me.

Margins:
The space that gives space,
    lends openness,
        invites notations.

Margins:
The space on the fringes,
    not quite included,
        definitely not in.

Margins:
The space beyond traditional text,
    nudging suspicion,
        raising eyebrows.

Margins:
The space delegated to the unwanted,
    those labeled misfits,
        those not in.

Margins:
The space receptive to the Spirit,
    ready for God's grace,
        hungry for God's Word.

Oxygen and Such

July 2002

It sounded so selfish:
"In an emergency, when the oxygen masks drop,"
    directed the flight attendant,
  "put on your own mask first.
    Then help your child."
My inner voice screamed, "But my child?!
  My child needs my help."
Then came the realization:
  Without oxygen for myself,
    I would be unable to help my child.
That truth carries through for ministry.
Only with plenty of "oxygen"
  will I be able to minister to others.
I can share only that which I have to give.
Before I can accompany others
  on their spiritual journeys,
  I must be deeply rooted
    in my relationship with God.
Teaching the faith will bear fruit
  only if my faith is integral to my life.

My words will be but clanging cymbals
  unless they are founded in the Word.

When others are hurting, as so many are,
    I can apply healing balm
        only after attending
        to my own woundedness.
Forgiveness can flow only from awareness
    of my acceptance of forgiveness
        from God, self, and others.
Facing my own inclination to sin
    tempers my readiness
        to stand in judgment of others.
Embracing my Lord's love for me
    enables me to radiate that love
        to my sisters and brothers.
Breathing deeply of the "oxygen"
    of wholesome self-care
        is anything but selfish,
    for then, and only then, is it possible
        to minister effectively
            in the name of the Spirit of Love.
"To keep a lamp burning,"
    Mother Teresa tells us,
    "we need to keep putting oil in it."
Lamps need oil.
    Flames need oxygen.

Bumping Places

August 2009

Two friends,
    recounting their spiritual journeys—
        the glories, the excitement, the ecstasy
           of God's embrace—
        intertwined with the accounts of bumping places—
        the disappointments, the frustrations,
           the crunches of life,
           of relationships—

Bumping places that disrupt
    the peaceful current,
        the flow of delight.
Bumping places that arouse doubts:
    What is life all about?
    How can it be so?
Bumping places that necessitate a deeper look,
    stronger conviction,
        greater discernment.
Bumping places that require divine intervention,
    that unlock God-given passion
        for what is true.

Bumping places that plunge to the depths:
    Where is God directing?
    What is the loving response?
    How to be faithful
        to one's Faithful God
        while being bombarded
        with conflicting theologies
        and contradicting voices?

Two friends,
    growing in awareness
        that bumping places
    are integral
        to growth,
        to the spiritual journey.

The Cupboard of Socks

June 2002

I reached up, with both hands,
    to open the cupboard doors –
        a goodly sized cupboard –
    to find it stuffed with socks.

Socks? Why socks?

The dream tantalized me
    until it released its secrets:
Decades of voices screaming,
        "Stuff it!"
        "Put a sock in it!"

Subtle, sometimes blatant voices taunted,
        "It's futile. No one will hear you."
        "You don't know what you're talking about."
            "Don't sass your mother."
            "Rome has spoken."
            "You're only a woman."
            "You're only a lay minister."
            "They'll only laugh at you."

Sort out those socks.
      Shake them free.
Give voice –
    your God-given voice –
    to your truth – grace-fully –
    truth afire with the Spirit.

Sea of Pink

February 2011

During our Mission Awareness Trip
    in Trichy, India,
from our place of honor—
    a makeshift stage
        on colorful plastic chairs—
we sponsors look out to behold a sea of pink.

Five thousand mothers sitting cross-legged
        on the dusty ground
each with silky black hair
    pulled back in a bun,
each with black eyes sparkling
    in anticipation and gratitude,
each holding private stories
    of hardship and pain,
each in an identical pink sari
    to accentuate equality
        one with the other.

This pink sea
　　　shines calm and motionless,
　　yet a powerful undercurrent
　　　of love and determination stirs
　　these mostly illiterate mothers
　　　to transform their lives
　　from poverty to potential.

CHAPTER 4

SEASONS AND CELEBRATIONS

Tongues of fire appeared, which parted and came to rest on each of them.

Acts 2:3

Echoing

Becoming a Cowstall

Advent 2004

If you could turn your heart into a cowstall,
    Christ would be born again on earth. *

A cowstall in a cave,
    rustic and strong,
        hewn by Carpenter's hands,
    stands accepting and receptive,
        offering protection and nurturance—
so that Christ can be born again on earth.
The cowstall of the heart,
    authentic and pure,
        hewn by the Creator's Hands,
    stands accepting and receptive,
        offering compassion and peace—
so that Christ can be born again on earth.
The cowstall of the Church,
    far-reaching and holy,
        hewn of all God's people,
    stands accepting and receptive,
        offering welcome and Eucharist—
so that Christ can be born again on earth.

*   Angelus Silesius, *The Soul Is Here for Its Own Joy*

✣ ✣ ✣

Echoing

Turning toward Resurrection

Lent 2005

"Repent!" Jesus proclaimed.
"Turn around!
Turn to *ME*
    with your whole heart.
Turn and look deep within.
    Permit *ME* to wipe away your fears and doubts.
    Allow *ME* to fill you with peace.
Turn and look around.
    Find *ME* in every person you meet.
    Allow *ME* to radiate through you.
Turn from the dust and ashes of sin.
    Permit *ME* to wash you clean.
    Allow *ME* to clothe you in love.
Turn from the grave of death.
    Permit *ME* to loosen the shroud that binds you.
    Allow *ME* to swaddle you
        in *MY NEW LIFE*."

✡ ✡ ✡

Jubilee

February 2000

JUBILEE seems such a FOREIGN notion
in today's rush-around world.
Yet, a look *within* reveals FAMILIARITY
with its RECURRING RHYTHMS—
time and timelessness,
doing and being,
wealth and sharing,
working and resting,
inward rituals and outward action.

JUBILEE—FOREIGN, yet as FAMILIAR
as six days of LABOR
and a day of REST,
as bodily RHYTHMS
that are the CYCLE of LIFE.

JUBILEE bids us WORK and REST,
PRODUCE and lie FALLOW,
GARNER and SHARE,
FORGIVE and allow FORGIVENESS,
LABOR for LIBERTY,
relentlessly SEARCH for RELEASE
for OURSELVES and OTHERS.

JUBILEE bestows FRUITION
    only after a time of RESTORATION,
    necessitates CLOSURE for what HAS BEEN
    while begging BLESSINGS for NEW BEGINNINGS,
      bids the extension of GOD'S FORGIVENESS
        to forgiveness of SELF and OTHERS,
    deepens roots in internal AWARENESS of RHYTHMS
    in preparation of BLOSSOMING RITUALS without.

JUBILEE invites TRUST
    in our GOD's BOUNDLESS LOVE.

✼ ✼ ✼

Echoing

Metanoia

September 2006

Metanoia! Repent!

"Meta" = change
"Noia" = mind, soul, life

The Prophets cry, "Repent!"
John the Baptist cries,
    "Prepare the way of the Lord!"

We live as though in a cave.
We see as in the darkness.
Our shadow is our reality.
Turn to the Light!

The Light beckons, "Turn to Me!
    I am the Way, the Truth, the Light."

In Anticipation Of Commissioning

(Mark 12:15)

November 1998

Through a lifetime of ministry
    it has been my privilege to teach
        and to have been taught much more.
In awe, I have journeyed with others
    through their joys and sorrows,
        only to find still others who cared for me.
Humbled by the request to be spiritual guide,
    I, too, have been lovingly
        guided through life's paths.

No mere words can describe the power,
    the awesome responsibility
        of that deep knowing of God's call,
"Go into the whole world
    and proclaim the good news
    to all creatures."

Blessings beyond number
    reassure me of God's affirmation.
Gratitude expressed by God's people as they
    "grow in wisdom, age, and grace"
        validate my response to God's call
        to proclaim, " OUR God loves you!"

Though first commissioned at my Baptism,
    and having been enriched
        by a multitude of experiences,
    I rejoice as I anticipate the day when the Church
      openly and readily recognizes
    what God has already begun in me—
      and in a whole multitude of lay ministers—
    and commissions me/us to go forth
      to continue to proclaim God's love.

By God's love and grace,
    we will continue to enrich the Church
      even as we are enriched.

Echoing

Marriage Matters

August 2004

On their wedding day each vows, "I do!"
Each day of their marriage
    they strive toward, "We do!"
"For better and for worse…"
    "I do." "We do."
They come as two to become one,
       yet maintain
    their individual, unique identities.
It is said he is from Mars,
      she from Venus,
    each with ingrained approaches
       to life and expression.
Ah, the challenge to speak and listen,
    to hear and to respond lovingly.
Bodies and spirits complement each other,
    bringing gift and challenge.
Created in love by their God
    they mirror God's gracious love
    in their lovemaking.
In word, in action, in spirit
    husband and wife channel
    God's grace to each other,
      and to others.

✻ ✻ ✻

CHAPTER 5

LIVING WITH CANCER

*Suddenly from up in the sky came a noise like a strong driving wind,
which was heard all through the house where they were seated.*

Acts 2:2

The Sentence

June 2010

The doctor approached
    having just viewed the X-ray.
Calmly he reports, that midafternoon, 3/10/10,
    "Your heart is fine.
    The spot on your lung
        is bigger than in 2006."
"What spot?"
    Stunned silence.
CT scan verifies the probability of cancer.

That simple sentence,
    softly, professionally spoken
        by the doctor with a Jewish name,
is now a sentence of harsh reality—
    long procession of doctors and tests,
    surgical removal of spot-toting lobe,
    rigors of chemotherapy
        with stomach-curdling nausea,
    dulled taste buds
        reduce eating to a chore,
    lagging energy.

Ah, the battle among
    TRUST: I know God is with me.
    FEAR: How to decide with wisdom?
        What are the consequences?
            For me? For Harv?
    DISCOURAGEMENT:
        Is it all really necessary?
        When will it end?
        Why such uncertain outcomes?
    LOVE: Lavished abundantly from hearts of care.
I want my life back!

Why did Jesus have to go ahead
    and drink His Cup dry?
Yet, RESURRECTION triumphs
    over struggle and death.

Aching

July 2010

The diagnosis is lung cancer,
   and the empty space
      of the missing lobe in my chest
   prickles as it readjusts to new alignment.
Yet, it's the aching in the pit of my gut—
   brought on by chemo
      designed to get rid
      of any wandering, unwanted invaders
      while bestowing unwelcome side effects—
that persists, torments, yearns to be filled
      while being repulsed at the thought
        of taking in anything new,
   wanting to be left alone
      while craving to be satisfied,
   needing to be fed
      while turning away from nourishment,
   dreading more discomfort
      while knowing there is more to come.

How I long to feel good—really good—again!

Alongside the deep peace
    of God's ever-loving presence
my spirit is aching,
yearning for my old life back
while realizing there must be
    something new around the corner,
craving wisdom in the midst of untold uncertainty,
seeking direction while floundering with questions:
    Are there secrets they aren't telling us?
    Will the cancer metastasize,
        as its name suggests?
    Will radiation be helpful, or do damage?

My body, my soul, my spirit are aching—
    even as God is with me.
My God is ever faithful.
    I yearn to know how to be faithful in return.

Echoing

A Year or Two

September 2010

The doctor was nudging me
    to a more practical reality—
instead of ten years longer to live
    "think a year or two."

A year or two?

Just a year or two?
    How can that be true?
The possibility hardly seems real.
    True, I have cancer,
        but I don't feel that sick.
As a matter of fact,
    I feel pretty darn good
        for all I've been through.
A bit of neuropathy in my feet
    pokes at my disbelief
and arouses more questions:
    What other symptoms await me?
A year or two?
    And how many more?
        Or less?

What am I to do—
    except to live my life as fully as I can,
    love as best as I know how,
    let my God and others love me
    and proclaim that love
        for as long as I live.

✳ ✳ ✳

Echoing

The Incision

2010

The setting is Sunday Liturgy
shortly after my lung surgery.
As the Eucharistic Cup is lifted high
a quickening of my spirit
unites me with the Blood of Christ
soon to be poured out.
Simultaneously, the incision in my side,
still tender from the chest tube,
chafes under my feminine support garment,
pressing, rubbing,
irritating the deepening scar,
arousing sacred connections.
The Eucharistic Mystery
mingles physical distress
with spiritual yearning
for greater recognition of the gaping incision
in the side of Mother Church
inflicted by those who fail to acknowledge
the feminine gifts
readily available and eager,
though not readily utilized,
to enhance the Kingdom.

✡ ✡ ✡

My Ministry—Today

October 2010

As I headed for "my" chair in the chemo room
    "Cathy" spotted me and determined
        that we would chat.
    I had hoped to lose myself in a crossword puzzle.
Straightforward and with vibrancy in her voice
    Cathy tells of being in chemo treatment
        for eight years.

EIGHT YEARS! The possibility strikes fear in my soul.
    The eight months—so far—
        has seemed an eternity.
EIGHT YEARS! No way! There's no way!
    Please, God! Not me! Not that long!

Yet, how long will it take for this endeavor?
The uncertainties of journeying with cancer
        are legion and looming.

There are no certainties!
    The doctors attend to multiple concerns,
        and yet they offer no certitudes.
    Will the reports show progress this time?
    What if the scans disclose more tumors?
    How will my body respond
        to even more harsh chemicals?
    What will happen to Harv? To us?

Grappling with medical uncertainties
        entails grappling with my ministry.
    What is my ministry NOW—TODAY?
Glimpses, a word here, a comment there
    suggest that others are deeply moved
        as they consider the reflections I offer.

Amid all the uncertainties and concerns
    I realize TODAY my ministry is to be faithful
        to the God who is forever faithful to me,
    and to reflect that faithfulness to others
        while living with my traveling companion—
        lung cancer.

The Gift of Swallowing

November 2010

The "knot" in my throat verifies the doctor's prediction:
    radiation so close to the esophagus
        does cause discomfort when swallowing.
    How does one live if one can't swallow?
When had it ever occurred to me that
    being able to swallow was indeed a gift?
Soon the tightness and the knot in my throat
    made eating much less enjoyable.
What a temptation to forego food, even drink.
Yet, swallow I must,
    even as my musings deepened.
Is the knot trying to tell me something
        about other aspects of my life?

So many times I have chosen to swallow my words
    rather than arouse another's disapproval,
        or risk rebuke from authority,
            maybe even be silenced,
        rather than speak my truth.
How often have I deferred to another's word
    rather than trust my own?

Far too often I swallowed my anger
    rather than find a wholesome expression.

Yet, there are blessings in this journey.
Facing my mortality as never before,
      I sense a new, more vibrant inner spirit.
    One that nudges me to LIVE as fully as I can.
    One that encourages me
      to SPEAK my truth in PEACE.
    One that energizes me
      to REACH OUT to others in LOVE.
    One that knows even more deeply
      that GOD is with me—ALWAYS!

Though my rejoicing will be great when my throat heals
      and the KNOT is untied,
    I hope that sometimes, when I SWALLOW
      I will be reminded
  that swallowing truly is a GIFT,
      a gift that helps to nourish my BODY
        and to enliven my SPIRIT.

Suzie the Bear

July 2011

Countless times, surrounded by the glorious Smokies,
     at the base of our driveway,
    I caught daily glimpses of Suzie the black bear,
      encaged in iron bars much too confining
        for a creature her size.
Encaged, deprived of the freedom to roam her beloved hills,
    forced to forego interaction with her own kind
      or stretching her legs,
    this beautiful creature was totally dependent
      for sustenance on a Cherokee man
        striving to win over a few tourist dollars.

In recent weeks a new response has come tumbling off my tongue
    in an effort to answer the repeated query,
      "How are you feeling today?"
    "I feel like a caged animal."
Shortness of breath creates the need to gasp for air.
    Lack of air and limited energy
      restrict my activity.
    Though my medical care is excellent
      much of my "social" life is limited
        to treatments and doctor appointments.

Suzie will never know her impact on my life.
　　Though thirty years span the time
　　　　since my last glimpse of her,
　　Her confinement afforded me the grace
　　　　to acknowledge some things
　　　　　in my life were unduly confining and stifling.

Continuing my journey with lung cancer,
　　today Suzie the Bear continues to nudge me
　　　　to better understand
　　what I am saying when
　　　　"I feel like a caged animal"
　　　　　tumbles from my lips.

CHAPTER 6

CLOSING VERSES

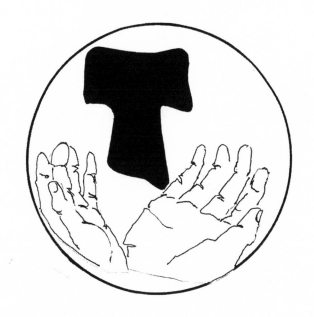

A Response to God's Echoing Call

July 2011

As I entered more deeply into Franciscan spirituality
    I was enamored by St. Francis'
        boundless expression of his love for God—
           and God's love for him.
One of his greatest yearnings
        was to be a Herald of the Great King.
    His desire became mine.
As did his plea in his Peace Prayer,
    "Lord, make an instrument of Your peace."

Using images for God that far exceed masculine and ruler,
    my soul thrives on proclaiming with Francis,
        "My God and my All."

Presenting this small volume is one of my opportunities
    to raise my voice to herald my ever-loving God.
In like mind I pray these reflections
    will serve as an "instrument of peace"
        to dispel some of the tension in our Church.

Our response to God's echoing call can easily
    be enfolded in Francis' Peace Prayer:

    Lord, make me an instrument of your peace;
    where there is hatred, let me sow love;
    where there is injury, pardon;
    where there is doubt, faith;
    where there is despair, hope;
    where there is darkness, light;
    and where there is sadness, joy.

    O, Divine Master,
    grant that I may not so much seek to be consoled
        as to console;
    to be understood as to understand;
    to be loved, as to love;
    for it is in giving that we receive,
    it is in pardoning that we are pardoned,
    and it is in dying that we are born to eternal life.

ENDORSEMENTS

Laughter, tears, and love dance in the lines and verses of *An Echoing Call*. Marcy shares her love of God and love of God's people with wisdom, honor, and the truths of the journey we call life. This book is a blessing to all who hear the echoing call of God to serve and love.

Bridget Thien, MDiv
Lutheran School of Theology at Chicago

As I read through this little book, I thought repeatedly of the spiritual writers of old—true saints of God, contemplatives, vessels of God's love—sharing His truth with fellow seekers, with the world. Truly, God's call to love is timeless. It still exists today—and it is proclaimed anew through this godly daughter of Christ. It is His wisdom, guidance, and insight shared through this charming, poignant, and inspiring little book. In *An Echoing Call*, Marcy Keefe-Slager shares her life with God, and inspires thereby a deeper understanding and a renewed commitment to live fully into our baptismal covenant—to follow our call to love God, and to love God's people. Her story will inspire, her book will enrich, and her message will encourage your life.

Rev. Thomas M. Ball, EdD, DMin
Elder, Southern Michigan Conference
Free Methodist Church of North America

I have known Marcy for over twenty years, first as spiritual director and mentor, then as friend. In this collection of poems she expresses her deep faith and her passion for God, ministry, and church. In doing so she raises her voice and joins the ranks of women who call upon the Catholic Church to dialogue about their role. May her voice be heard and live on.

Dr. Patricia Robertson
Author of *Daily Meditations (with Scripture) for Busy Moms*

If you are looking for someone who understands what it is like to face serious struggles in life, you will find that person in the pages of this book. Through beautiful prose Marcy Keefe-Slager tells of roadblocks that have threatened to hinder her from living out God's call in her life. But she doesn't stop there. When people, policies, and physical health threaten her, Marcy shares how the love of God frees, sustains, and gives her peace and joy. As you follow her journey, you will find refreshing honesty and deep wisdom. This book will speak to your spirit and refresh your soul.

Mary Albert Darling
Coauthor of *The God of Intimacy and Action* and *Connecting Like Jesus*
Associate Professor of Communication and Spiritual Formation
Spring Arbor University

Women called by God to be ministers continue to struggle with religious structures that restrict and a culture that pulls us backward. Even so, God gifts us with courageous women like Marcy Keefe-Slager who is pastor, priest, anointed, ordained, and made holy by God's spirit. Often women are ordained to ministry solely by the Spirit of God. As Marcy shares in her poetry, such women have found creative ways to lift their voices, and to use their bodies to be the presence of God in our midst. We need these voices and the sometimes-unsettling process that brings them to dare speak on God's behalf.

Marcy's voice is one of unlimited and unconditional grace. She stands in a great cloud of witnesses, shouting a resounding "yes!" to our God who is for her, through her, with her, in her, and is more fully present on earth because of her. Entering Marcy's journey through poetry engages us in our own journeys to give voice to God calling to the world through us. Her book will appeal to the spiritual journeys of men and women, Protestant and Catholic, and all those who seek the hope of God.

Rev. Gretchen C. Sanewsky
Pastor, First Baptist Church
Jackson, Michigan

ARTIST ELISE COLE

Elise B. Cole has been creating art since childhood. She attended art classes at the Buffalo Museum of Science and went on to achieve a BS in Design from the University of Michigan. Elise has worked in printmaking, drawing, painting, and fabric. She is a daughter, sister, wife, mother, and granny. After additional study at the Whitaker School of Theology, Elise was ordained a Deacon of the Episcopal Church of America.

ARTWORK: *PARABLES*

The inspiration for each piece of artwork was derived from the contents of the chapter (or book) and the portion of Scripture presented with it. Each of the passages from Scripture is a personification of the Holy Spirit. The Presence of the Holy Spirit was part of each poem—each poem was spoken from Marcy's heart. Truly, the Spirit has led us to choose those various Scriptures.

NOTES